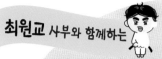

최원교 사부와 함께하는

태권영어 교실

최원교 사부와 함께하는

태권영어교실

최원교 지음

이담
Books

영어를 잘 하려면 여러 가지가 갖추어져야 한다. 회화도 잘 해야 하고 문법도 알아야 하고 발음도 좋아야 하고 단어도 많이 외워야 한다. 하지만 영어를 처음 접하는 어린이나 초등학생들은 먼저 영어라는 외국어와 친해져야 한다.

이 책은 실제 태권도장에서 이루어지는 상황들을 간단한 대화로 엮어 수련생들이 영어에 흥미를 가질 수 있게 꾸몄다. 또한 교육부에서 선정한 '초등학생이 꼭 알아야 할 영어단어'도 수록하였다. 세계태권도연맹에서 규정한 동작들을 저자의 제자들을 통해 시범을 보인 사진을 실어서, 태권도를 수련 중인 수련생들에게 올바른 태권도 동작을 알려주고자 했다.

태권도를 사랑하는 어린이들의 심리를 학습 과정에 응용하여 되도록 쉽고 재미있게 공부할 수 있도록 꾸몄다. 총 20가지 주제를 하루에 하나씩 익히면 한 달만에 기본적인 영어 회화를 어렵지 않게 구사할 수 있을 것이다.

이 책은 태권도를 주제로 한 국내 최초의 영어 학습서이다. 아직도 부족한 부분이 있겠지만, 이 책이 태권도를 수련 중인 어린이들의 영어 교육에 많은 도움이 되기를 기대한다. 더불어 글로벌 시대를 사는 우리 어린이들의 미래가 더 넓게 열리기를 기원한다.

2008년 12월

최원교

차 례

CONTENTS

CONTENTS

01

운동 중 부상
(An injury during the exercise)

chapter 1

운동 중 부상
(An injury during the exercise)

태권도 규정동작

① 나란히서기　② 앞서기

A : What happened, Jun-hee?

B : I think I've sprained my ankle.

A : Are you okay?

B : I don't think I can exercise Taekwondo anymore.

A : Let's go to see a doctor.

B : I hope it's not a serious injury.

본문해석

A : 무슨 일이니, 준희야?

B : 다리가 삔 것 같아.

A : 괜찮니?

B : 더 이상 태권도를 할 수 없겠어.

A : 의사 선생님께 가보자.

B : 중상이 아니면 좋겠는데.

다음 문장을 큰 소리로 읽고 따라 쓰세요.

A : What happened, Jun-hee?

_____

B : I think I've sprained my ankle.

_____

A : Are you okay?

_____

B : I don't think I can exercise Taekwondo anymore.

_____

A : Let's go to see a doctor.

_____

B : I hope it's not a serious injury.

_____

ankle : 발목	sprain : 삐다	think : 생각하다
Let's : ~하자	go : 가다	see : 보다
serious : 심각한	injury : 상해, 손상	hope : 바라다, 원하다

우리말과 같은 뜻이 되도록 영어 문장을 완성하세요.

01 What _____, jun-hee?

(무슨 일이니, 준희야?)

02 I think _____ ankle.

(다리가 삔 것 같아.)

03 _____ okay?

(괜찮니?)

04 I _____ taekwondo anymore.

(더 이상 태권도를 할 수 없겠어.)

05 Let's go to _____.

(의사 선생님께 가보자.)

06 I _____ a serious injury.

(중상이 아니면 좋겠는데.)

쪽지시험

1. think   •   •   A. 바라다

2. hope   •   •   B. 심각한

3. serious   •   •   C. 생각하다

계 절

January	[dʒǽnjuèri / -əri]	1월
February	[fébruèri, fébrju- / fébruəri]	2월
March	[maːrtʃ]	3월
April	[éiprəl]	4월
May	[mei]	5월
June	[dʒuːn]	6월
July	[dʒuːlái]	7월
August	[ɔ́ːgəst]	8월
September	[səptémbər]	9월
October	[aktóubər / ɔk-]	10월
November	[nouvémbəːr]	11월
December	[disémbər]	12월
season	[síːz-ən]	계절
spring	[spriŋ]	봄
summer	[sʌ́mər]	여름
autumn	[ɔ́ːtəm]	가을
winter	[wíntəːr]	겨울

태권도 규정동작

나란히서기 Naranhi seogi
(Parallel stance)

규정동작 Movement

가. 두 발 사이는 한 발바닥 길이의 너비로 하며 발의 안쪽(발날등)은 서로 나란히 한다.
나. 두 다리의 무릎은 편다.
 a. The breadth of two feet will be one foot wide, the inner sides(Balnaldeung) of both feet paralleling with each other.
 b. Both knees are stretched.

감점동작의 예 Deduction Factors

가. 발 앞 끝이 오므려지거나 열려 있을 때.
나. 이 밖에 규정동작이 아닌 행위는 감점이 된다.
 a. Tip of the feet are closed or open.
 b. Any other movements other than shown above will be factors of deduction.

앞서기 Ap seogi
(Walking stance)

규정동작 Movement

가. 걸어가다 멈췄을 때의 한 걸음 길이로 선다.
나. 두 무릎은 펴며 체중을 두 다리에 균일하게 실어야 한다.
다. 몸통을 반듯하게 세우고 정면을 향한 가슴을 30% 정도 자연스럽게 틀어준다.
 a. Just like the stance when one stops walking with a forward step. The distance of the two feet is one step long.
 b. The inner sides of two feet must be on a straight line.
 c. The body should be straightened while facing forward. The chest should be turned about 30 degrees. The weight should be supported by both legs evenly.

감점동작의 예 Deduction Factors

가. 보폭이 너무 넓거나 너무 좁을 때.
나. 몸이 뒤로 젖혀지는 경우.
다. 이 밖에 규정동작이 아닌 행위는 감점이 된다.
 a. Stride of the step is too long or short.
 b. Body is leaning Back.
 c. Any other movements other than shown above will be factors of deduction.

실수
(Making mistakes)

태권도 규정동작
앞굽이 (Forward inflection stance)

chapter 2

실수
(Making mistakes)

태권도 규정동작

❶ 앞굽이

A : The door is broken.

B : How did it happen?

A : I broke it by mistake.

B : Haven't you hurt yourself?

A : I said frankly to the master.
He said he would fix it after the exercise.

B : Everyone makes mistakes.

본문해석

A : 문이 부서졌어.

B : 어떻게 이런 일이 생겼니?

A : 실수로 내가 부쉈어.

B : 다치지는 않았니?

A : 사부님께 말씀드렸어. 운동 후 수리하신대.

B : 누구나 실수는 하기 마련이야.

다음 문장을 큰 소리로 읽고 따라 쓰세요.

A : The door is broken.

_____

B : How did it happen?

_____

A : I broke it by mistake.

_____

B : Haven't you hurt yourself?

_____

A : I said frankly to the master.

He said he would fix it after the exercise.

_____

B : Everyone makes mistakes.

_____

Key Expressions

door: 문   broke: 깨다, 부수다   happen: 일어나다
mistake: 실수   exercise: 운동, 연습
frankly: 솔직히   fix: 고정시키다, 갖다 붙이다
hurt: 다치게 하다, 아프게 하다

우리말과 같은 뜻이 되도록 영어 문장을 완성하세요.

01 The _____ is broken.
(문이 부서졌어.)

02 _____ happen?
(어떻게 이런 일이 생겼니?)

03 I broke it _____.
(실수로 내가 부쉈어.)

04 _____ you hurt yourself?
(다치지는 않았니?)

05 I said _____ master.
(사부님께 말씀드렸어.)

06 He said he would fix it _____.
(운동 후 수리하신대.)

07 Everyone _____.
(누구나 실수는 하기 마련이야.)

쪽지시험

1. door   •

2. happen   •

3. fix   •

• A. 고정시키다

• B. 문

• C. (사건이) 일어나다

가 족

family	[fǽməli]	가족
home	[houm]	집, 가정
parent	[pɛ́ərənt]	부모
father	[fáːðər]	아버지
mother	[mʌ́ðəːr]	어머니
grandfather	[grǽndfáːðər]	할아버지
grandmother	[grǽndmʌ́ðər]	할머니
brother	[brʌ́ðər]	형, 오빠, 남동생
sister	[sístəːr]	언니, 자매, 여동생
son	[sʌn]	아들
daughter	[dɔ́ːtər]	딸
cousin	[kʌ́zn]	사촌
uncle	[ʌ́ŋkəl]	백부, 숙부
aunt	[ænt / aːnt]	이모, 숙모

앞굽이 Ap kubi
(Forward inflection stance)

규정동작 Movement

가. 두 발의 간격은 한 걸음 반 정도로 한다. 앞발 끝과 뒷발 끝은 한 발바닥 길이의 너비로 한다.

나. 앞발의 발끝이 앞을 향하게 선다.

다. 몸을 반듯하게 하고 서서 땅을 내려다봤을 때 앞에 있는 무릎과 발끝이 일치되도록 무릎과 몸을 낮춘다.

라. 뒷발의 내각이 30° 이내가 되게 선다. 뒷다리의 무릎을 펴며 체중의 2/3를 앞에 둔다.

마. 몸을 반듯하게 세우고 몸통은 앞쪽으로 30° 정도로 튼다.

a. The vertical distance between two feet is one and a half step. And the parallel distance between two feet's tiptoes is one foot.

b. The tiptoes of front foot place forward.

c. lower the knee in order to match your knee and tiptoes when you look down in a upright standing position.

d. keep the back sole turned inward within the angle of 30 degrees and stretch the knee of hind leg and pet the balance of your weight forward by two-thirds.

e. Stand upright and twist forward your body at an angle of 30 degrees.

감점동작의 예 Deduction Factors

가. 보폭이 넓어 허리와 골반부가 서기 균형을 이루지 못할 때.

나. 뒤축이 들리거나 뒷무릎이 굽어질 때.

다. 뒷발이 30° 이상 벌어질 때.

라. 중심이 앞으로, 또는 뒤로 쏠릴 때.

a. Between the two feet is too wide so without keep the body balance.

b. Lift of heel the front foot or bend of back leg.

c. Back of foot is opened more then 30 degree.

d. Center of the balance keep the front part of the body.

03

도장합숙

(Training camp at the gym)

태권도 규정동작

뒷굽이 (Backward inflection stance)

도장합숙
(Training camp at the gym)

태권도 규정동작

❶ 뒷굽이

A : Hey, everyone, I've heard good news.
  The master would hold a training camp this coming Saturday.

B : Great! Where is it going to be held?

A : At the Taekwondo gym.

B : Good! Do you know what the camp training program would be?

A : He said it's going to be a fun game camp training.

본문해석

A : 얘들아, 반가운 소식이 있어.
  이번 주 토요일에 사부님께서 합숙을 하신대.

B : 와! 어디서 하는데?

A : 태권도장에서.

B : 좋아! 합숙 프로그램이 뭐니?

A : 재미있는 게임 합숙이래.

다음 문장을 큰 소리로 읽고 따라 쓰세요.

A : Hey, everyone, I've heard good news.

The master would hold a training camp this

coming Saturday.

B : Great! Where is it going to be held?

A : At the Taekwondo gym.

B : Good! Do you know what the camp training

program would be?

A : He said it's going to be a fun game camp training.

Key Expressions

hear: 듣다   good: 좋은   training: 훈련, 연습
news: 뉴스   gym: 체육관   know: 알다, 이해하다
fun: 재미있는   camp: 캠프

우리말과 같은 뜻이 되도록 영어 문장을 완성하세요.

01 Hey, everyone, I've heard _____.
(얘들아, 반가운 소식이 있어.)

02 The master would hold a training camp
_____.
(이번 주 토요일에 사부님께서 합숙을 하신대.)

03 Great! _____ going to be held?
(와! 어디서 하는데?)

04 At the _____.
(태권도장에서.)

05 _____.
(좋아!)

06 _____ what the camp training program
would be?
(합숙 프로그램이 뭐니?)

07 He said it's going to be a _____.
(재미있는 게임 합숙이래.)

쪽지시험

1. gym •   • A. 체육관

2. fun •   • B. 알다

3. know •   • C. 재미있는

색깔

color	[kʌ́lər]	색
white	[hwait]	흰색
black	[blæk]	검정
yellow	[jélou]	노랑
blue	[bluː]	파랑
red	[red]	빨강
green	[griːn]	녹색
pink	[piŋk]	분홍
brown	[braun]	갈색
gray	[grei]	회색
gold	[gould]	금색, 금
silver	[sílvəːr]	은색, 은

뒷굽이 Dwitkubi
(Backward inflection stance)

규정동작 Movement

가. 모아서기에서 오른빌 뒤축을 축으로 잎축을 90° 되게 벌려 선다.

나. 오른발을 90° 벌려 선 상태에서 왼발 한 걸음 길이로 앞으로 내디디며 몸을 반듯하게 세우고 두 무릎을 굽혀 몸을 낮춘다.

다. 몸을 낮출 때 오른다리 무릎은 오른발 끝 방향으로 지면과 60~70° 되게 충분히 굽히고 왼다리 무릎은 정면(왼발 끝 방향)으로 지면에서 100~110°가량 되게 약간 구부린다. 역시 두 무릎도 90°가 되게 하여야 한다. 앞주춤서기 때와 같이 무릎을 안으로 조이면 안 된다.

a. From the moaseogi(Close stance), the fore sole or right foot is opened at angle of 90 degrees, pivoting on the back sole.

b. Then the left foot is put one step forward from the heel of the right foot, making an angle of 90 degrees and the body is lowered by the inflection of two knees.

c. The inflection of the right foot knee will keep an angle of 60 to 70 degrees between the ground and the shin and the inflection of the left foot knee an angle of 100 to 110 degrees the ground and the left shin the two knees inwardly like the ap juchumseogi.(forward riding stance)

감점동작의 예 Deduction Factors

가. 뒷무릎이 열릴 때.
나. 중심이 앞으로 쏠릴 때.
다. 앞발 뒤꿈치가 들릴 때.
라. 엉덩이가 뒤로 빠지면서 범서기 같은 형태가 될 때.
마. 이 밖에 규정동작이 아닌 행위는 감점이 된다.

a. Knee of the back leg is open backwards.
b. Body weight is leaning forward.
c. Heel of the front foot is raised.
d. Hips are pulled back and stance becomes similar to BeomSeogi.(Tiger Stance)
e. Any other movements other than shown above will be factors of deduction.

04

집합
(Gathering)

태권도 규정동작
오른서기 (Right hand stance)
왼서기 (Left hand stance)

chapter 4

집합
(Gathering)

태권도 규정동작

❶ 오른서기   ❷ 왼서기

A : Everyone, come here! Let's start today's exercise.

Sit up straight. What do I have here?

B : Fun king cards.

A : You can leave them with your master for a while.

Take them after the exercise.

B : Okay.

본문해석

A : 집합, 운동 시작하자.

정좌. 내가 가지고 있는 물건은 무엇이니?

B : 유희왕 카드입니다.

A : 사부님에게 잠시 맡겨두도록 하자.

운동 끝나고 가져가.

B : 예.

다음 문장을 큰 소리로 읽고 따라 쓰세요.

A : Everyone, come here! Let's start today's

exercise. Sit up straight.

What do I have here?

B : Fun king cards.

A : You can leave them with your master for

a while.

Take them after the exercise.

B : Okay.

우리말과 같은 뜻이 되도록 영어 문장을 완성하세요.

01 _____ Let's start today's exercise.
(집합, 운동 시작하자.)

02 _____ straight.
(정좌.)

03 _____ have here?
(내가 가지고 있는 물건은 무엇이니?)

04 Fun _____.
(유희왕 카드입니다.)

05 You can leave them with your master
_____.
(사부님에게 잠시 맡겨두도록 하자.)

06 Take them _____.
(운동 끝나고 가져가.)

07 _____.
(예.)

교 통

bus	[bʌs]	버스
taxi	[tǽksi]	택시
subway	[sʌ'bwèi]	지하철
train	[trein]	열차
plane	[plein]	비행기
ship	[ʃip]	배
boat	[bout]	작은 배
bicycle	[báisikəl]	자전거
truck	[trʌk]	트럭, 화물차

태권도 규정동작

오른서기 Oreun seogi
(Right hand stance)

규정동작 Movement

가. 나란히 서기와 모두 같으나 다만 왼발은 제자리, 오른발은 틀어 앞축을 90°로 돌려 딛는다.
  a. First, take the same pose as the naranhi seogi and then only the fore sole of right foot 90 degrees right-wards, pivoting on the heel.

감점동작의 예 Deduction Factors

가. 나란히 서기로 섰을 때.
나. 발을 모아 섰을 때.
다. 이 밖에 규정동작이 아닌 행위는 감점이 된다.
  a. Standing in Naranhi seogi.
  b. Placing feet together.
  c. Any other movements other than shown above will be factors of deduction.

왼서기 Wen seogi
(Left hand stance)

규정동작 Movement

가. 나란히 서기와 모두 같으나 다만 오른발은 제자리, 왼발은 틀어 앞축을 90°로 돌려 딛는다.
  a. First, take the same pose as the naranhi seogi and then move only the fore sole of left foot 90 degrees left-wards, pivoting on the heel.

감점동작의 예 Deduction Factors

가. 오른서기 감점동작과 동일.
나. 이 밖에 규정동작이 아닌 행위는 감점이 된다.
  a. Same as the deduction factors of the Oreun seogi.
  b. Any other movements other than shown above will be factors of deduction.

05

연습
(Practice)

chapter 5

연습
(Practice)

태권도 규정동작

① 뒤꼬아서기　② 앞꼬아서기　③ 곁다리서기　④ 오금서기

A : What are you good at?

B : I'm good at Taekwondo.

A : Oh, are you?

B : Yes, I'm getting better.

A : Practice makes perfect, as you know.

B : That's right. I agree with you.

본문해석

A : 너는 무엇을 잘하니?

B : 태권도를 잘해.

A : 태권도 잘하니?

B : 응, 점점 나아지고 있어.

A : 알다시피 연습하면 완벽해져.

B : 맞아, 그런 것 같아.

다음 문장을 큰 소리로 읽고 따라 쓰세요.

A : What are you good at?

_____

B : I'm good at Taekwondo.

_____

A : Oh, are you?

_____

B : Yes, I'm getting better.

_____

A : Practice makes perfect, as you know.

_____

B : That's right. I agree with you.

_____

better: 더 좋은   practice: 연습   right: 옳은, 바른

perfect: 완벽한   agree: 동의하다

우리말과 같은 뜻이 되도록 영어 문장을 완성하세요.

01 _____ good at?

(너는 무엇을 잘하니?)

02 I'm good at _____.

(태권도를 잘해.)

03 Oh, _____?

(태권도 잘하니?)

04 Yes, I'm getting _____.

(응, 점점 나아지고 있어.)

05 _____, as you know.

(알다시피 연습하면 완벽해져.)

06 _____. I agree with you.

(맞아, 그런 것 같아.)

쪽지시험

1. agree •   • A. 연습, 훈련

2. practice •   • B. 완벽한

3. perfect •   • C. 동의하다

공간

place	[pleis]	장소, 위치
house	[haus]	집, 가옥
gate	[geit]	문, 출입문
door	[dɔːr]	문
hall	[hɔːl]	현관, 홀
window	[wíndou]	창문
room	[ruːm / rum]	방
kitchen	[kítʃin]	부엌
floor	[flɔːr]	마루
stair	[stɛəːr]	계단
roof	[ruːf / ruf]	지붕
wall	[wɔːl]	벽
bridge	[bridʒ]	다리
hospital	[háspitl / hɔ́s-]	병원
church	[tʃəːrtʃ]	교회

1. 뒤꼬아서기 Dwikkoa seogi (Backward cross stance)
: 앞으로 접근하거나 짓찧기할 때 사용한다.

2. 앞꼬아서기 Apkkoa seogi
   (Forward cross stance)
   : 몸을 옆으로 이동할 때 사용한다.

3. 곁다리서기 Kyotdari seogi
   (Assisting stance)

4. 오금서기 Ogeum seogi
   (Reverse crane stance)
   : 학다리서기와 같으나 중심을
     지지하는 발 오금에 반대 발
     발등을 가볍게 붙인다.

날씨
(Weather)

태권도 규정동작
범서기 (Tiger stance)

chapter 6

날씨
(Weather)

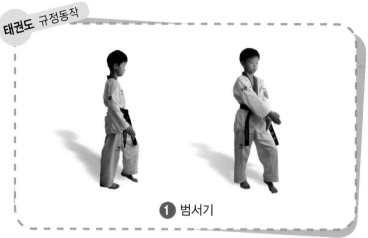

① 범서기

A : What's the weather like outside?

B : It's warm.

A : Do you like this kind of weather?

B : Yes, I like warm days.

A : It's a fine day.

I think I will be able to do exercise better today.

본문해석

A : 바깥 날씨 어떠니?

B : 따뜻해요.

A : 이런 날씨 좋아하니?

B : 예, 저는 따뜻한 날이 좋아요.

A : 날씨 좋은 날이다.

운동이 더욱 잘되겠는걸.

다음 문장을 큰 소리로 읽고 따라 쓰세요.

A : What's the weather like outside?

_____

B : It's warm.

_____

A : Do you like this kind of weather?

_____

B : Yes, I like warm days.

_____

A : It's a fine day.

_____

I think I will be able to do exercise better today.

_____

weather: 날씨   warm: 따뜻한
outside: 바깥, 외부   fine: 맑은, (날씨 등이) 쾌청한

우리말과 같은 뜻이 되도록 영어 문장을 완성하세요.

01 What's the weather _____?

(바깥 날씨 어떠니?)

02 It's _____.

(따뜻해요.)

03 _____ this kind of weather?

(이런 날씨 좋아하니?)

04 Yes, I like _____.

(예, 저는 따뜻한 날이 좋아요.)

05 It's a _____.

(날씨 좋은 날이다.)

06 I think I will be able to do exercise

_____. (운동이 더욱 잘되겠는걸.)

쪽지시험

1. warm •   • A. 날씨

2. fine •   • B. 따뜻한

3. weather •   • C. 맑은, 쾌청한

자 연

river	[rívəːr]	강
wood	[wud]	나무, 목재
tree	[triː]	나무
hill	[hil]	언덕
lake	[leik]	호수
ground	[graund]	땅, 운동장
plant	[plænt / plaːnt]	식물
rock	[rak / rɔk]	바위
stone	[stoun]	돌
sun	[sʌn]	태양
cloud	[klaud]	구름
rain	[rein]	비
snow	[snou]	눈
shower	[ʃáuəːr]	소나기
earth	[əːrθ]	지구

범서기 Beom seogi
(Tiger stance)

규정동작 Movement

가. 모아서기에서 오른발을 30° 정도의 각으로 넓혀 서며 왼발을 오른발 끝에서 한 발바닥 길이로 내딛는다.

나. 체중을 뒷발에 싣고 뒷발을 내려다봤을 때 무릎과 발끝이 일직선이 되게 한다.

다. 앞에 있는 왼발의 발목을 펴고 발끝 또는 앞축만 가볍게 딛고 무릎을 약간 안으로 튼다.

라. 아랫배에 힘을 주며 체중을 뒷발에 90~100% 싣는다.

a. From the position of Moaseogi, the left foot is put one foot forward. And the right(hind) foot is opening the fore sole 30 degrees on the basis of the back sole.

b. The weight is entirely supported by the right(hind) foot behind. Place th knee and tiptoes match when you look down.

c. The left foot in front will keep the ankle stretched so that its tiptoes or the fore sole alone may lightly touch the ground and the knee will bend down as it is required.

d. Concentrate the force on the lower abdomen, the weight is supported 100% by the right(hind) foot.

감점동작의 예 Deduction Factors

가. 무릎이 열릴 때.

나. 보폭이 너무 짧거나 길 때.

다. 상체가 뒤로 젖혀지거나 또는 엉덩이가 과도하게 뒤로 빠질 때.

라. 이 밖에 규정동작이 아닌 행위는 감점이 된다.

a. Knees are open.

b. Stride of the step is too long or short.

c. Hips are pulled back or upper body is leaning forward.

d. Any other movements other than shown above will be factors of deduction.

07

따라 하기
(Imitating movements)

태권도 규정동작

모아서기 (Close stance)

주춤서기 (Riding stance)

chapter 7

따라 하기
(Imitating movements)

❶ 모아서기　　❷ 주춤서기

A : Let's learn a new way of kicking.

B : Yes, master.

A : Today, you're going to learn how to jump high and kick toward the front.

B : Isn't it too difficult?

A : Don't worry. You can do it.

B : Okay.

본문해석

A : 모두 새로운 발차기를 배워 보자.

B : 예, 사부님.

A : 오늘은 높이 뛰어 앞차기를 알려줄게.

B : 너무 어렵지 않나요?

A : 걱정하지 마라. 너희들은 할 수 있을 거야.

B : 예.

○ 다음 문장을 큰 소리로 읽고 따라 쓰세요.

A : Let's learn a new way of kicking.

_____

B : Yes, master.

_____

A : Today, you're going to learn how to jump

_____

high and kick toward the front.

_____

B : Isn't it too difficult?

_____

A : Don't worry. You can do it.

_____

B : Okay.

_____

우리말과 같은 뜻이 되도록 영어 문장을 완성하세요.

01 Let's learn a new way of _____.
(모두 새로운 발차기를 배워 보자.)

02 Yes, _____.
(예, 사부님.)

03 Today, you're going to learn how to _____ toward the front.
(오늘은 높이 뛰어 앞차기를 알려줄게.)

04 Isn't it _____ difficult?
(너무 어렵지 않나요?)

05 _____. You can do it.
(걱정하지 마라. 너희들은 할 수 있을 거야.)

06 _____.
(예.)

쪽지시험

1. learn •   • A. 높은

2. high •   • B. 걱정

3. worry •   • C. 배우다

음 식

food	[fuːd]	음식
dish	[diʃ]	접시
spoon	[spuːn]	숟가락
knife	[naif]	칼
chicken	[tʃíkin]	닭고기
salad	[sǽləd]	샐러드
egg	[eg]	달걀
rice	[rais]	밥, 쌀
bread	[bred]	빵
dessert	[dizə́ːrt]	후식
milk	[milk]	우유
water	[wɔ́ːtəːr / wɑ́t-]	물
glass	[glæs / glɑːs]	유리
ice	[ais]	얼음
cake	[keik]	케이크

태권도 규정동작

1. 모아서기 Moa seogi
(Close stance)

규정동작 Movement

가. 두 발날등을 맞대고 서며 두 무릎을 곧게 편다.
  a. Stand upright with both inner feet blades attached and stretch both knees.

감점동작의 예 Deduction Factors

가. 발 앞 끝이 열려 있을 때.
나. 이 밖에 규정동작이 아닌 행위는 감점이 된다.
  a. Tip of feet are open.
  b. Any other movements other then shown above will be factors of deduction.

2. 주춤서기 Juchum seogi
(Riding stance)

규정동작 Movement

가. 발과 발의 너비가 두 발바닥 길이 정도로 선다.
나. 발의 안쪽(발날등)이 서로 나란히 되게 한다.
다. 몸통은 반듯하게 하고 두 무릎을 굽히는데, 서서 땅을 내려다봤을 때 무릎과 발끝이 일치되도록 한다.
라. 무릎은 안으로 조이듯 한다.
  a. Keep the breadth of two legs two foot length.
  b. The two soles paralleling with each other.
  c. Lower the knees as high as they may spring up and down easily. and keep the shin from shin from the foot to the knee erect vertically.
  d. Concentrating the weight inwardly and tightening the lower abdomen.

감점동작의 예 Deduction Factors

가. 무릎이 열리거나 닫힐 때.
나. 발끝이 오므려지거나 열릴 때.
다. 엉덩이가 뒤로 빠지거나 상체가 앞으로 쏠릴 때.
라. 이 밖에 규정동작이 아닌 행위는 감점이 된다.
  a. Knees are open or closed.
  b. Tip of the feet are closed or open.
  c. Hips are pulled back or upper body is leaning forward.
  d. Any other movements other than shown above will be factors of deduction.

아픈 친구
(Sick friend)

태권도 규정동작
학다리서기 (Crane stance)

태권도 규정동작

1 학다리서기

A : Gil-dong is absent from the Taekwondo class today.

B : I've heard that he's in the hospital.

A : Really?

B : Yes.

I heard it from his mom herself in the morning.

A : Oh, that's why he got two hours off from the school yesterday.

본문해석

A : 길동이 오늘 태권도 수업 결석이야.

B : 입원해 있대.

A : 정말이니?

B : 그래.

아침에 길동이 엄마께 직접 들었어.

A : 그래서 어제 학교에서 두 시간 일찍 조퇴했구나.

다음 문장을 큰 소리로 읽고 따라 쓰세요.

A : Gil-dong is absent from the Taekwondo class today.

_____

B : I've heard that he's in the hospital.

_____

A : Really?

_____

B : Yes.

I heard it from his mom herself in the morning.

_____

A : Oh, that's why he got two hours off from the

school yesterday.

_____

absent: 결석   class: 학급, 반   hear: 듣다

hospital: 병원   school: 학교

우리말과 같은 뜻이 되도록 영어 문장을 완성하세요.

01 Gil-dong is _____ the Taekwondo class today.
(길동이 오늘 태권도 수업 결석이야.)

02 I've heard that he's _____.
(입원해 있대.)

03 Really?
(정말이니?)

04 Yes.
(그래.)

05 _____ from his mom herself in the morning.
(아침에 길동이 엄마께 직접 들었어.)

06 Oh, that's why he got _____ from the school yesterday.
(그래서 어제 학교에서 두 시간 일찍 조퇴했구나.)

쪽지시험

1. class •   • A. 학급

2. hear •   • B. 듣다

3. school •   • C. 학교

시 간

time	[taim]	시간
o'clock	[əklák / əklɔ́k]	～시
morning	[mɔ́ːrniŋ]	아침
afternoon	[æ̀ftərnúːn / àːf-]	오후
A. M.	[eiem]	오전
P. M.	[piːem]	오후
evening	[íːvniŋ]	저녁
night	[nait]	밤
today	[tədéi / tu-]	오늘
tonight	[tənáit / tu-]	오늘 밤
year	[jiəːr / jəːr]	연, 나이
month	[mʌnθ]	월, 달
week	[wiːk]	주, 일주일
day	[dei]	날, 하루
holiday	[hálədèi / hɔ́lədèi]	휴일

태권도 규정동작

학다리서기 Hakdari seogi (Crane stance)
: 반대 발의 발날등을, 중심을 지탱하는 발 무릎에 가볍게 붙인다.

규정동작 Movement

가. 중심 발은 주춤서기 높이.
나. 반대 발은 발날등을 무릎 안쪽에 붙인다(무릎을 벌려서는 안 되며, 붙이는 발은 지면에서 들어 바로 무릎 안쪽에 붙인다).
  a. The height of the Crain stance should be same as the riding stance.
  b. The reverse foot blade raise to inner part of the knee. (Do not open the knee, the closing of the knees should be towards the inside of the knee.)

감점동작의 예 Deduction Factors

가. 서기에서 무릎이 퍼지는 경우(중심 발).
나. 반대 발이 지지축 무릎에 붙지 않은 경우.
다. 학다리서기를 일부러 천천히 하는 행위.
라. 이 밖에 규정동작이 아닌 행위는 감점이 된다.
  a. Keep knee straight for Crain stance.
  b. The reverse foot of the Crain stance must not touch the opposite leg.
  c. The reverse foot of the Crain stance should be moved slowly.
  d. Any movements other than shown above will be deduction points.

화장실
(Toilet)

태권도 규정동작
아래막기 (Low blocking)

chapter 9

화장실
(Toilet)

태권도 규정동작

❶ 아래막기

A : Where are you going?

B : To the toilet.

A : Hurry up. It's almost time for the exercise.

B : Okay, I'll be back soon.

Would you please keep a seat for me?

A : Okay, I will.

본문해석

A : 어디 가니?

B : 화장실에.

A : 빨리 와. 운동시간 거의 다 됐어.

B : 알았어, 곧 돌아올게.

내 자리 좀 맡아줄래?

A : 그래.

다음 문장을 큰 소리로 읽고 따라 쓰세요.

A : Where are you going?

_____

B : To the toilet.

_____

A : Hurry up. It's almost time for the exercise.

_____

B : Okay, I'll be back soon.

_____

Would you please keep a seat for me?

_____

A : Okay, I will.

_____

toilet: 화장실   hurry: 서두르다   seat: 자리

almost: 거의, 대부분   keep: 보존하다, 간직하다

우리말과 같은 뜻이 되도록 영어 문장을 완성하세요.

01 _____ going?

(어디 가니?)

02 To the _____.

(화장실에.)

03 Hurry up. _____ for the exercise.

(빨리 와. 운동시간 거의 다 됐어.)

04 Okay, I'll be _____.

(알았어, 곧 돌아올게.)

05 _____ keep a seat for me?

(내 자리 좀 맡아줄래?)

06 Okay, _____.

(그래.)

사람들

people	[píːpl]	사람들
baby	[béibi]	아기
kid	[kid]	아이
child	[tʃaild]	아이
boy	[bɔi]	소년
girl	[gəːrl]	소녀
man	[mæn]	남자
woman	[wúmən]	여자
student	[stjúːd-ənt]	학생
author	[ɔ́ːθər]	작가
friend	[frend]	친구
guest	[gest]	손님
citizen	[sítəzən]	시민
thief	[θiːf]	도둑
devil	[dévl]	악마

아래막기 Arae makki
(Low blocking)

규정동작 Movement

가. 막는 주먹은 앞발의 대퇴부에서 세운 주먹 두 개 또는 한 뼘 정도의 간격이다.

나. 반대 팔목은 젖힌 주먹으로 장골능에 위치 시킨다.

[요령] 막는 주먹은 어깨 높이 정도 올리고 막는 주먹 바닥 부분이 반대편 얼굴을 향하 게 한다. 반대 손은 엎은 주먹 상태로 뻗어 명치 선에 오게 한다. 막는 팔의 팔꿈치가 들리지 않아야 하며 몸에 붙지 않는 선에 서 행한다.

a. The blocking fist is to be kept apart from the thigh of the fore-leg by the width of two fists.

b. The wrist of the hand will rest on the waist side in the form of bending.

[Point of attention] The blocking fist will be lifted up to the shoulder's level and the base part of the fist will face the opposite side of the face. The other hand will be stretched toward the pit of stomach in a stare of bent wrist. The elbow of the blocking arm will be lifted up nor stuck to the body.

감점동작의 예 Deduction Factors

가. 막는 팔이 바깥에서 나오는 경우.

나. 반대 손을 당기기 전 팔이 구부러진 상태에 서 당기는 경우.

다. 동체를 과장되게 틀어서 막는 경우.

라. 막는 팔이 무릎까지 오지 않거나 벗어나는 경우.

마. 막았을 때 막는 팔의 팔꿈치가 구부러지는 경우.

바. 시작 단계에 막는 팔의 팔꿈치가 들리는 경우.

사. 이 밖에 규정동작이 아닌 행위는 감점이 된다.

a. Blocking arm is coming from outward.

b. Bending the arm before and after pulling.

c. Exaggerated twist of the body.

d. Blocking arm not going all the way to the knee or going over.

e. Banding the elbow of the blocking hand when blocking.

f. Lifting the elbow of the blocking arm.

g. Any other movements other than shown above will be factors of deduction.

생일선물
(Birthday present)

태권도 규정동작
몸통막기 (Body blocking)

chapter 10

생일선물
(Birthday present)

태권도 규정동작

① 몸통막기

A : Today is my birthday.

B : Congratulations!

A : Thank you.

B : Today is your day.

What kind of exercise do you want to practice?

A : I'd like to play a game.

B : Okay, today we're going to play a game for exercise.

본문해석

A : 오늘이 제 생일이에요.

B : 축하해.

A : 고맙습니다.

B : 오늘은 너의 날이다. 운동 뭐 하고 싶니?

A : 게임하고 싶어요.

B : 알았다, 오늘 운동수업은 게임이다.

다음 문장을 큰 소리로 읽고 따라 쓰세요.

A : Today is my birthday.

_____

B : Congratulations!

_____

A : Thank you.

_____

B : Today is your day.

_____

What kind of exercise do you want to practice?

_____

A : I'd like to play a game.

_____

B : Okay, today we're going to play a game for exercise.

_____

today: 오늘   birthday: 생일   want: 원하다

play: 놀다, 장난하다   practice: 연습, 숙련

우리말과 같은 뜻이 되도록 영어 문장을 완성하세요.

01 Today is _____.
(오늘이 제 생일이에요.)

02 _____.
(축하해.)

03 _____.
(고맙습니다.)

04 Today is _____.
(오늘은 너의 날이다.)

05 _____ exercise do you want to practice?
(운동 뭐 하고 싶니?)

06 I'd like to _____.
(게임하고 싶어요.)

07 _____, today we're going to play a
game for exercise.
(알았다, 오늘 운동수업은 게임이다.)

쪽지시험

1. birthday •   • A. 원하다

2. play •   • B. 놀다

3. want •   • C. 생일

기 분

joy	[dʒɔi]	기쁨
anger	[ǽŋgər]	노여움
hope	[houp]	희망
dream	[driːm]	꿈
love	[lʌv]	사랑
peace	[piːs]	평화
mood	[muːd]	기분
danger	[déindʒər]	위험
advice	[ædváis / əd-]	충고
care	[kɛər]	근심, 걱정
pardon	[páːrdn]	용서
hurry	[həˊːri / hʌˊri]	서두름
alarm	[əlaˊːrm]	놀람, 경보
wonder	[wʌˊndəːr]	놀라움

몸통막기 Momtong makki (Body blocking)

규정동작 Movement

가. 모든 몸통막기는 손목이 몸의 중앙에 와야 한다.
나. 팔꿈치의 각도는 90°~120° 정도 벌린다.
다. 막는 주먹은 어깨 높이로 한다.
라. 막는 손목이 구부러지지 않아야 한다.
마. 반대 손목은 젖힌 주먹으로 장골능에 위치 시킨다.

a. In all the torso-inner blocking the hand and the wrist must be kept at center of the body.
b. The elbow is to be kept around 90~120 degrees.
c. The blocking fist is kept as high as the shoulder.
d. the blocking wrist should not be bent.
e. The non-blocking hand should be kept at the side of the waist, in a form of a bent fist.

감점동작의 예 Deduction Factors

가. 막는 팔이 몸의 중심선보다 더 들어올 때 (덜 들어올 때도).
나. 막기가 시작될 때, 막는 팔의 팔꿈치가 과도하게 들리거나 팔목이 어깨보다 낮게 들어올 때.
다. 이 밖에 규정동작이 아닌 행위는 감점이 된다.

a. Blocking arm going further inside then the center line of the body.
b. Lifting the elbow of the blocking arm too high or putting the wrist below the shoulder when starting the block.
c. Any other movements other than shown above will be factors of deduction.

운동 중 휴식
(Break during the exercise)

태권도 규정동작

얼굴막기 (Face blocking)

chapter 11

운동 중 휴식
(Break during the exercise)

태권도 규정동작

1 얼굴막기

A : Aren't you tired? Let's take a ten-minute break.

B : Thank you.

A : (A moment later) Everyone, gather around.

B : Pardon?
Has the break finished already?

A : How many minutes have passed?

B : Just five minutes, sir.

본문해석

A : 힘들지? 10분간 휴식.

B : 감사합니다.

A : (잠시 후) 집합.

B : 예?
벌써 쉬는 시간이 끝났어요?

A : 지금 몇 분 지났지?

B : 이제 겨우 5분 지났습니다.

다음 문장을 큰 소리로 읽고 따라 쓰세요.

A : Aren't you tired? Let's take a ten-minute break.

_____

B : Thank you.

_____

A : (A moment later) Everyone, gather around.

_____

B : Pardon?

Has the break finished already?

_____

A : How many minutes have passed?

_____

B : Just five minutes, sir.

_____

우리말과 같은 뜻이 되도록 영어 문장을 완성하세요.

01 Aren't you tired? Let's _____.
(힘들지? 10분간 휴식.)

02 _____.
(감사합니다.)

03 (A moment later) Everyone, _____.
((잠시 후) 집합.)

04 _____?
(예?)

05 _____ finished already?
(벌써 쉬는 시간이 끝났어요?)

06 How many minutes have _____?
(지금 몇 분 지났지?)

07 Just _____, sir.
(이제 겨우 5분 지났습니다.)

쪽지시험

1. finish •   • A. 이미

2. already •   • B. 끝내다

3. tire •   • C. 피곤하다

수련용어

grand master	[grænd] [mǽstəːr / máːstəːr]	관장
master	[mǽstəːr / máːstəːr]	사범
uniform	[júːnəfɔ̀ːrm]	도복
color belt	[kʌ́lər] [belt]	유급자
black belt	[blæk] [belt]	유단자
basic form	[béisik] [fɔːrm]	기본동작
form	[fɔːrm]	품새
sparring	[spáːriŋ]	겨루기
one-step sparring	[wʌ́n-stèp] [spáːriŋ]	약속겨루기
self-defence technique	[sélf-diféns] [tekníːk]	호신술
breaking	[bréikiŋ]	격파
demonstration	[dèmənstréiʃən]	시범
competition	[kámpətíʃən / kɔ̀m-]	시합

태권도 규정동작

얼굴막기 Olgul makki
(Face blocking)

규정동작 Movement

가. 막는 팔의 팔목이 얼굴 중앙선에 오게 한다.

나. 막는 팔목은 이마에서 세운 주먹 하나 정도 떨어지게 한다.

다. 반대 손목은 옆구리(장골능)에 위치한다.
[요령] 막는 팔은 젖힌 주먹으로 반대 팔 팔꿈치보다 약간 바깥쪽 아래로 하고, 반대 팔은 주먹 등이 위를 향하게 하여 반대편 어깨 높이에서 시작한다.

a. The wrist of the blocking arm comes right in front of the center of the face.

b. The blocking wrist is one fist's distance apart from the forehead.

c. The other had's wrist is situated at the waist side.
[Point of attention] The blocking arm should be kept slightly lower than the outside of the arm's elbow and the other arm starts from the shoulder's hight of the other side, keeping the fist directed upward.

감점동작의 예 Deduction Factors

가. 막는 팔목의 중심선이 얼굴의 중심선 바깥으로 벗어나거나 이마 뒤로 넘어갈 때.

나. 막는 팔을 과장되게 휘둘러서 들어올 때.

다. 이 밖에 규정동작이 아닌 행위는 감점이 된다.

a. Wrist of the blocking arm going out of the center line of face or going over the forehead.

b. Lifting the blocking arm with exaggerated swing.

c. Any other movements other than shown above will be factors of deduction.

화장실이 어디예요?
(Where is a toilet?)

태권도 규정동작

몸통바깥막기 (Outer body blocking)

화장실이 어디예요?

(Where is a toilet?)

태권도 규정동작

❶ 몸통바깥막기

A : Where is a toilet?

B : It's at the end of the corridor.

A : Thank you.

B : May I help you find the toilet?

A : Yes, please.

본문해석

A : 화장실이 어디에 있니?

B : 복도 끝에 있어.

A : 고마워.

B : 화장실 찾는 것 도와줄까?

A : 응, 부탁할게.

다음 문장을 큰 소리로 읽고 따라 쓰세요.

A : Where is a toilet?

_____

B : It's at the end of the corridor.

_____

A : Thank you.

_____

B : May I help you find the toilet?

_____

A : Yes, please.

_____

Key Expressions

end: 끝   corridor: 복도

find: 찾아내다, 발견하다

우리말과 같은 뜻이 되도록 영어 문장을 완성하세요.

01 _____ a toilet?

(화장실이 어디에 있니?)

02 It's at the end of _____.

(복도 끝에 있어.)

03 _____.

(고마워.)

04 May I help you _____?

(화장실 찾는 것 도와줄까?)

05 Yes, _____.

(응, 부탁할게.)

쪽지시험

1. corridor •

2. find •

3. end •

 • A. 찾아내다

 • B. 끝

 • C. 복도

수련용어

warming up	[wɔ́ːrmiŋ] [ʌ́p]	준비운동
cooling down	[kuːliŋ] [daun]	정리운동
meditation	[mèdətéiʃ-ən]	명상
attention	[əténʃən]	차렷
bow	[bàu]	경례
ready	[rédi]	준비
begin/go	[bigín] / [gou]	시작
stop	[stap / stɔp]	바로
turn to left	[təːrn] [tuː] [left]	좌향좌
turn to right	[təːrn] [tuː] [rait]	우향우
face to face	[féis] [tuː] [féis]	좌우향우
stand up	[stǽnd] [ʌp]	일어서
sit down	[sít] [dàun]	앉아
lie on back	[lai] [ɔːn] [bæk]	누워

몸통바깥막기 Momtong bakkat makki
(Outer body blocking)

규정동작 Movement

가. 막는 주먹 등이 몸으로 향하게 하고 주먹
   끝이 어깨선과 일치하게 한다.

나. 반대 손목은 옆구리 장골능에 위치시키고,
   주먹 바닥이 위를 향하게 한다.
   [요령] 막는 팔의 주먹은 젖힌 주먹으로 반
   대 팔의 팔꿈치보다 약간 아래(주먹 하나
   정도)에 두고, 반대 팔은 막는 팔 안쪽에서
   주먹 등 부분이 위쪽을 향하게 하여 막는 팔
   의 어깨에서 약간 떨어진 상태로 시작한다.

a. The blocking fist must be directed
   toward the body and the end of the fist
   must be parallel with the shoulder line.

b. The outer hand's wrist should be situated
   at the waist side, the bottom of the fist kept
   faced upward.
   [Point of attention] The fist of the blocking
   arm, in form of bending backward, is kept
   slightly lower(one fist's distance) than the
   other arm's elbow, and the other arm is
   kept slightly apart from the blocking arm's
   shoulder, keeping the fist back directed
   from the inner side of the blocking arm.

감점동작의 예 Deduction Factors

가. 막았을 때 막는 팔이 몸통선 전이나 후에
   멈출 때(막는 동작이 작은 경우).

나. 막기가 시작될 때, 막는 팔의 팔꿈치가 과도하게
   들리거나 막는 팔목이 어깨보다 낮게 들어올 때.

다. 이 밖에 규정동작이 아닌 행위는 감점이 된다.

a. Stopping the block before blocking arm
   reaches the line of the shoulder.(Motion
   of the block is too small.)

b. The elbow of the blocking arm too high
   or putting the wrist below the shoulder
   when starting the block.

c. Any other movements other than shown
   above will be factors of deduction.

좋아하는 발차기
(Favorite kick)

태권도 규정동작

손날막기 (Knife hand blocking)

chapter 13

좋아하는 발차기
(Favorite kick)

태권도 규정동작

1 손날막기

A : I don't like taking exercises for physical strength.

B : Neither do I.

A : What's your favorite exercise?

B : Taekwondo. Especially, I like kicking.

A : I like all movements.

I like trunk reverse punch the most.

본문해석

A : 체력운동은 정말 하기 싫어.

B : 나도 그래.

A : 좋아하는 운동은 무엇이니?

B : 태권도. 특히 발차기를 좋아해.

A : 난 다 좋아해.

특히 품새를 제일 좋아하지.

다음 문장을 큰 소리로 읽고 따라 쓰세요.

A : I don't like taking exercises for physical strength.

_____

B : Neither do I.

_____

A : What's your favorite exercise?

_____

B : Taekwondo.

_____

Especially, I like kicking.

_____

A : I like all movements.

_____

I like trunk reverse punch the most.

_____

physical: 신체의   strength: 힘, 체력

favorite: 특별히 좋아하는   especially: 특히

movement: 운동, 활동

우리말과 같은 뜻이 되도록 영어 문장을 완성하세요.

01 _____ taking exercises for physical strength.
(체력운동은 정말 하기 싫어.)

02 _____ do I.
(나도 그래.)

03 What's your _____?
(좋아하는 운동은 무엇이니?)

04 _____.
(태권도.)

05 _____, I like kicking.
(특히 발차기를 좋아해.)

06 I like _____.
(난 다 좋아해.)

07 I like _____ the most.
(특히 품새를 제일 좋아하지.)

쪽지시험

1. favorite •   • A. 특히 좋아하는

2. physical •   • B. 특히

3. especially •   • C. 신체의

신체용어

face	[feis]	얼굴
eye	[ai]	눈
nose	[nouz]	코
mouth	[mauθ]	입
ear	[iər]	귀
brow	[brau]	이마
head	[hed]	머리
neck	[nek]	목
chest	[tʃest]	가슴
trunk	[trʌŋk]	몸통
arm	[aːrm]	팔
elbow	[élbou]	팔꿈치
leg	[leg]	다리

손날막기 Sonant makki
(Knife hand blocking)

규정동작 Movement

가. 막는 손날의 위치는 몸통의 측면과 일치한다.
나. 손끝은 어깨 높이로 한다.
다. 손목이 구부러지지 않아야 하며 손바닥이 정면을 향하게 한다.
라. 거드는 손은 팔목이 명치 앞에 오게 하며 손날과 몸통 사이는 약간(손바닥 하나 사이) 띄워준다.

[요령] 막는 손은 손바닥을 위로 향하게 하고 반대 손은 손바닥 부분을 뒤로 향한 상태에서 시작한다. 반대 손의 손끝이 어깨선에 오고 팔꿈치를 약간 구부린 상태에서 자연스럽게 내리며, 막는 손은 손끝이 코앞을 지나가게 하고 거드는 손은 명치 쪽으로 당긴다.

a. The blocking hand-blade is located a position in parallel with the lateral part of the shoulder.
b. The finger-tips are kept as high as shoulder.
c. The wrist should not be bent, the palm facing the front.
d. The assisting hand should keep its wrist at a position in front of the stomach pit and the hand-blade slightly apart from the body.(The distance should be about half an inch apart).

감점동작의 예 Deduction Factors

(시작할 때)
가. 막는 팔이 머리와 어깨 사이 각을 벗어날 때.
나. 거드는 팔의 팔목이 몸통선 높이(장골능~어깨)를 벗어날 때.

(막았을 때)
가. 거드는 손의 손날이 팔목 중심선까지 오지 않을 때.
나. 막는 팔이나 거드는 팔의 팔꿈치가 바깥으로 들릴 때.
다. 이 밖에 규정동작이 아닌 행위는 감점이 된다.

(Beginning)
a. Blocking arm going out of the area between head and shoulder.
b. Assisting arm going out of the height of the body.(waist-shoulder)
(Blocking)
a. Knife hand of the assisting arm not reaching the center line of the wrist.
b. Elbows of the blocking arm and assisting arm are lifted outward.
c. Any other movements othe than shown above will be factors of deduction.

품새 습득 부탁

(Asking for help with practicing trunk reverse punch)

태권도 규정동작

바로지르기 (Regular punch)

반대지르기 (Reverse punch)

chapter 14

품새 습득 부탁

(Asking for help with practicing trunk reverse punch)

태권도 규정동작

① 바로지르기　　② 반대지르기

A : Have you finished learning trunk reverse punch this month?

B : No. I've still got a lot to learn.

It's too difficult.

A : Do you need my help?

B : Yes, I'll appreciate it if you help me.

A : Okay, what's the most difficult part to you?

본문해석

A : 이번 달 품새 다 배웠니?

B : 아니. 아직 멀었어.

너무 어려워.

A : 도움이 필요하니?

B : 응, 네가 도와주면 고맙겠어.

A : 좋아, 무엇이 문제야?

다음 문장을 큰 소리로 읽고 따라 쓰세요.

A : Have you finished learning trunk reverse

punch this month?

B : No. I've still got a lot to learn.

It's too difficult.

A : Do you need my help?

B : Yes, I'll appreciate it if you help me.

A : Okay, what's the most difficult part to you?

finish: 끝내다	learn: 배우다	month: 달, 1개월
need: 필요	help: 도움	difficult: 어려운
most: 가장 큰	appreciate: 고맙게 생각하다	

우리말과 같은 뜻이 되도록 영어 문장을 완성하세요.

01 Have you finished learning trunk reverse punch _____?
(이번 달 품새 다 배웠니?)

02 _____.
(아니.)

03 I've still got a lot to learn. _____.
(아직 멀었어. 너무 어려워.)

04 _____ my help?
(도움이 필요하니?)

05 Yes, _____ if you help me.
(응, 네가 도와주면 고맙겠어.)

06 Okay, what's _____ to you?
(좋아, 무엇이 문제야?)

쪽지시험

1. need   •   •   A. 가장 큰

2. learn   •   •   B. 배우다

3. most   •   •   C. 필요

신체용어

knee	[niː]	무릎
waist	[weist]	허리
hip	[hip]	엉덩이
groin	[grɔin]	낭심
hand	[hænd]	손
foot	[fut]	발
wrist	[rist]	손목
ankle	[ǽŋkl]	발목
finger	[fíŋgər]	손가락
fist	[fist]	주먹
hand knife	[hænd] [naif]	손날
heel	[hiːl]	발뒤꿈치
instep	[ínstèp]	발등
inside foot	[ínsáid] [fut]	발바닥

태권도 규정동작

바로지르기 Baro jireugi
(Regular punch)

규정동작 Movement

가. 서기의 다리를 앞뒤로 넓혀 딛고서(앞굽이, 뒷굽이 관계없이) 뒤에 있는 다리 쪽의 주먹으로 지르기를 하였을 때를 말한다. [요령] 당기는 주먹은 지르는 주먹의 목표와 같은 선상에서 당긴다.

a. When the feet are widely opened fore and back due to the movement of body weight(whether it is apkubi or dwitkubi), a baro Jireugi is performed by the fist on the side of the back foot. [Point of attention] The pulling fist will be pulled back through the same line with the target of the punching fist.

감점동작의 예 Deduction Factors

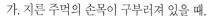

가. 지른 주먹의 손목이 구부러져 있을 때.
나. 지른 주먹 쪽의 팔꿈치가 구부러져 있을 때.
다. 예비동작이나 상체의 반동으로 지르는 경우.
라. 지르는 팔의 팔꿈치가 들려 나가는 경우.
마. 이 밖에 규정동작이 아닌 행위는 감점이 된다.

a. Wrist of the punching arm is bent.
b. Elbow of the punching arm is bent.
c. Punching with preliminary motion or bounce of the upper body.
d. Doing the motion of the punch with lifted elbow.
e. Any other movements other than shown above will be factors of deduction.

반대지르기 Bandae jireugi
(Reverse punch)

규정동작 Movement

가. 서기의 다리 중 앞에 있는 다리 쪽의 주먹으로 지르기를 하였을 때를 말한다.
   [요령] 당기는 주먹은 지르는 주먹의 목표와 같은 선상에서 당긴다.

a. A bandae jireugi is applied by the fist on the fore foot side, in the same situation as the above.
   [Point of attention] This pulling fist will be pulled back though the same line with the target of the punching fist.

감점동작의 예 Deduction Factors

가. 지른 주먹의 손목이 구부러져 있을 때.
나. 지른 주먹 쪽의 팔꿈치가 구부러져 있을 때.
다. 예비동작이나 상체의 반동으로 지르는 경우.
라. 지르는 팔의 팔꿈치가 들려 나가는 경우.
마. 이 밖에 규정동작이 아닌 행위는 감점이 된다.

a. Wrist of the punching arm is bent.
b. Elbow of the punching arm is bent.
c. Punching with preliminary motion or bounce of the upper body.
d. Doing the motion of the punch with lifted elbow.
e. Any other movements other than shown above will be factors of deduction.

15

승급시험
(Advancement test)

태권도 규정동작
몸통지르기 (Body punch)
얼굴지르기 (Face punch)
옆지르기 (Side punch)

승급시험
(Advancement test)

태권도 규정동작

① 몸통지르기　　② 얼굴지르기　　③ 옆지르기

A : Have you passed the advancement test this month?

B : Yes, I have.

A : Congratulations!
What did the master ask you about?

B : He asked me about 'kicking terms' in English.

A : It was a tough question. What about you?

B : Well, he asked me to say "what is your belt color?" in
English.

본문해석

A : 이번 달 승급시험 합격했니?

B : 응, 합격했어.

A : 축하해! 사부님이 무엇을 물어보셨니?

B : '발차기 용어'를 영어로 물어보셨어.

A : 어려웠어?

B : 응, 나한테 "당신의 띠 색깔은 무엇입니까?" 를 영어로 물어보셨어.

다음 문장을 큰 소리로 읽고 따라 쓰세요.

A : Have you passed the advancement test this month?

_____

B : Yes, I have.

_____

A : Congratulations!

_____

What did the master ask you about?

_____

B : He asked me about 'kicking terms' in English.

_____

A : It was a tough question. What about you?

_____

B : Well, he asked me to say

_____

"what is your belt color?" in English.

pass: 통과, 합격하다   advancement: 승진, 출세
test: 시험   tough: 곤란한, 힘든
question: 질문   ask: 묻다, 질문하다

15. 승급시험 **97**

우리말과 같은 뜻이 되도록 영어 문장을 완성하세요.

01 _____ the advancement test this month?

(이번 달 승급시험 합격했니?)

02 Yes, _____.

(응, 합격했어.)

03 _____! What did the master ask you about?

(축하해! 사부님이 무엇을 물어보셨니?)

04 _____ about 'kicking terms' in English.

('발차기 용어'를 영어로 물어보셨어.)

05 It was a tough question. _____?

(어려웠어?)

06 Well, he asked me to say " _____ " in English.

(응, 나한테 "당신의 띠 색깔은 무엇입니까?"를 영어로 물어보셨어.)

쪽지시험

1. tough   •   •   A. 질문

2. question   •   •   B. 시험

3. test   •   •   C. 곤란한

서기동작

close stance	[klouz] [stæns]	모아서기
parallel stance	[pǽrəlèl] [stæns]	나란히서기
riding stance	[ráidiŋ] [stæns]	주춤서기
walking stance	[wɔ́ːkiŋ] [stæns]	앞서기
back stance	[bæk] [stæns]	뒷굽이서기
forward cross stance	[fɔ́ːrwəːrd] [krɔ́ːs] [stæns]	앞꼬아서기
tiger stance	[táigəːr] [stæns]	범서기
crane stance	[krein] [stæns]	학다리서기

태권도 규정동작

몸통지르기 Momtong jireugi
(Body punch)

가. 몸통의 대표적인 목표인 명치를 지를 때 사용
하고 명치와 일직선상에 주먹을 위치시킨다.
[요령]
- 어깨를 자연스럽게 펴고 지르는 주먹의
팔목을 허리(장골능 위쪽)에 위치시키며
팔꿈치를 자연스럽게 몸 쪽으로 붙인다.
- 겨드랑이가 벌어지지 않은 상태에서 허
리의 반동을 최대한 이용해 반대편 주먹
을 빠르게 당기며, 동시에 직선으로 양
어깨의 정중앙 명치 높이로 지른다.
- 당기는 주먹은 명치와 일직선상에서 빠
르게 당긴다.

a. The solar plexus is the typical point of
attack in the trunk.
[Point of attention]
- The shoulder ate kept wide open
and the wrist of the punching fist
will rest on the waist, the elbow
sticking spontaneously to the body.
- The arm-pit is kept closed, the fist of
the opposite side is pulled rapidly with
the maximum use of the repulsive
power of the waist and at the same
time a punching is directed toward the
height of the stomach-pit at the right
center of the shoulders of both sides.
- The pulling fist is drawn back rapidly on
the straight line with the stomach-pit.

가. 주먹이 목표와 일치되지 않을 때.
나. 허리를 구부리거나 젖혀서 지를 때.
다. 지르기 규정을 벗어났을 때.
라. 이 밖에 규정동작이 아닌 행위는 감점이
된다.

a. Fist is off the target.
b. Banding or leaning the back when punching.
c. Transgressing the regulations
of jireugi.
d. Any other movements other than
shown above will be factors of
deduction.

태권도 규정동작

얼굴지르기 Olgul jireugi
(Face punch)

규정동작 Movement

가. 얼굴과 대표적인 목표인 인중을 지를 때 사용하고 인중과 일직선상에 주먹을 위치시킨다.
[요령] 지르는 요령은 몸통지르기와 동일하다.

a. The philtrum(base of nose) is the typical target point in the face for jireugi.
[Point of attention] The way of punching is identical with that of a momtong jireugi.

감점동작의 예 Deduction Factors

가. 몸통지르기 감점동작과 같음.
나. 이 밖에 규정동작이 아닌 행위는 감점이 된다.

a. Same as the deduction factors of the Momtong jireugi.
b. Any other movements other than shown above will be factors of deduction.

옆지르기 Yop jireugi
(Side punch)

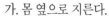

규정동작 Movement

가. 몸 옆으로 지른다.

나. 옆지르기는 주춤서기와 같이 두 발끝이 정면을 향할 때 행한다.

다. 주춤서기 자세로 주먹을 옆으로 지른다.
[요령] 몸통을 가로질러 있던 반대편 주먹을 당기며, 동시에 지르고자 하는 주먹을 옆으로 지른다.

a. One delivers a jireugi to his or her side.

b. A side-jireugi is executed when the two feet's tips are directed toward the front as in a juchumseogi stance.

c. The fist makes a jireugi sideways in juchumseogi stance.
[Point of attention] The fist on the other side which was crossing the trunk is pulled and at the same time, the punching fist makes a side jireugi.

감점동작의 예 Deduction Factors

가. 규정동작과 다를 때.

a. Different from the method of the movement.

16

야외수업
(Outdoor class)

chapter 16

야외수업
(Outdoor class)

태권도 규정동작

❶ 앞차기   ❷ 돌려차기   ❸ 옆차기

A : It's too noisy outside. Can you hear me?

B : No. I can't hear you well.

A : All right.

Can you hear me now?

B : Yes, we can.

A : Good, gather around.

본문해석

A : 밖이 너무 시끄럽군. 얘들아 사부님 말 잘 들리니?

B : 아뇨. 큰 소리로 말씀해 주세요.

A : 그래. 이제 들리니?

B : 네, 잘 들려요.

A : 좋아, 집합.

다음 문장을 큰 소리로 읽고 따라 쓰세요.

A : It's too noisy outside.

_____

Can you hear me?

_____

B : No. I can't hear you well.

_____

A : All right. Can you hear me now?

_____

B : Yes, we can.

_____

A : Good, gather around.

_____

noisy: 시끄러운   outside: 바깥쪽   hear: 듣다

now: 지금   gather: 모으다   around: 주위에

우리말과 같은 뜻이 되도록 영어 문장을 완성하세요.

01 It's _____ outside.
(밖이 너무 시끄럽군.)

02 Can you _____?
(얘들아 사부님 말 잘 들리니?)

03 _____.
(아뇨.)

04 _____ hear you well.
(큰 소리로 말씀해 주세요.)

05 _____.
(그래.)

06 Can you _____?
(이제 들리니?)

07 Yes, _____.
(네, 잘 들려요.)

08 Good, _____.
(좋아, 집합.)

쪽지시험

1. hear •   • A. 시끄러운

2. noisy •   • B. 듣다

3. gather •   • C. 모으다

막기동작

low blocking	[lou] [blákiŋ / blɔ́kiŋ]	아래막기
trunk/middle blocking	[trʌŋk] / [mídl] [blákiŋ / blɔ́kiŋ]	몸통막기
face/high blocking	[feis] / [hai] [blákiŋ / blɔ́kiŋ]	얼굴막기
knife hand blocking	[naif] [hænd] [blákiŋ / blɔ́kiŋ]	손날막기
scattered blocking	[skǽtəːrd] [blákiŋ / blɔ́kiŋ]	헤쳐막기
mountain shape blocking	[máunt-ən] [ʃeip] [blákiŋ / blɔ́kiŋ]	산틀막기
scissors blocking	[sízəːrz] [blákiŋ / blɔ́kiŋ]	가위막기
inward blocking	[ínwərd] [blákiŋ / blɔ́kiŋ]	안막기
outward blocking	[áutwərd] [blákiŋ / blɔ́kiŋ]	바깥막기
cross wrist blocking	[krɔːs / krɔs] [rist] [blákiŋ / blɔ́kiŋ]	엇걸어막기
forearm lunge blocking	[fɔ́ːràːrm] [lʌndʒ] [blákiŋ / blɔ́kiŋ]	거들어막기

앞차기 Ap chagi
(Front kick)

규정동작 Movement

가. 차는 다리의 무릎을 접어 끌어올려 가슴에 올 때 접었던 무릎을 펴면서 앞으로 내뻗는다. 발의 이동 궤도는 목표를 향하여 일직선이다.

나. 발가락을 젖힌 앞축으로 목표를 맞힌다.

다. 찬 발은 반작용으로 무릎을 접어 끌면서 먼저 자리에 놓는다.

라. 딛고 있는 다리는 차기 전이나 찬 후 무릎을 펴면 중심이 위로 떠서 힘이 약해져 넘어지기 쉽다. 또는 후속 조치를 취하기가 불리하다.

마. 딛고 있는 다리의 뒤축은 바닥에서 떨어지게 하고 앞축을 축으로 발바닥이 회전할 수 있도록 도와주었다가 차고 난 다음 다시 원위치로 돌아오게 한다.

a. Fist, raise the folded knee of the kicking leg up to breast and immediately push the foot forward, fully stretching the leg. The track of foot must be on a straight line toward the target.

b. The target must be kicked by the fore sole, the toes bending outward. The groin, lower part of abdomen, solar plexus, chin and etc. are the targets.

c. The kicking foot is drawn back by reaction to its original position. However, the foot may be placed where the attacker can easily make a next movement. If the attacker keeps himself out of balance while he or she executes a kicking or he or she retreats the kicking foot, the chagi was not perfect.

d. The supporting leg on the ground should not stretch the knee fully before or during the kicking because the upright standing is more likely to cause falling down of the attacker or weakening of the kicking force. Nor is easy to make next movement.

e. If the standing leg is supported by the entire sole of foot, the weight is laid on hip joint and the knee joint, in which case the kicking is less speedy and powerful of impulsive force. Sometimes, the knee joint or the hip joint breaks away. Therefore, it is necessary to lift the heel slightly by stretching the ankle so that fore sole may pivot at the moment of a kick and then the back sole will touch the ground again after the kick. However, one should be careful not to stretch the ankle too much, because if would lift up the center of weight.

감점동작의 예 Deduction Factors

가. 규정동작과 다를 때.
  a. Different from the method of the movement.

돌려차기 Dollyo chagi
(Roundhouse kick)

가. 앞의 축이 되는 발에 체중을 실어 차는 다리의 무릎을 접어 몸을 돌릴 때 접었던 무릎을 펴면서 발을 수평으로 돌려 앞축으로 상대의 목표를 가격한다(사용부위 앞축, 발등).

나. 축이 되는 다리는 무릎을 펴고 발목도 펴서 앞축을 축으로 몸의 회전이 잘되게 한다.

다. 찬 다리는 정한 목표에서 멈추어야 한다.

라. 돌려차기는 앞차기, 옆차기와 같이 궤도가 직선으로 이동하는 것이 아니다. 발을 몸 뒤에서 일단 올려 회전 이동한다.

마. 돌려차기를 많이 수련하면 차는 순간 발이 목표보다 약간 위에서 내리찍는 형태로 이루어지게 된다.

a. Putting the weight on the pivoting foot, one turns the body immediately after folding the knee and, as the knee stretches, makes the kicking foot circle horizontally so that the fore sole may kick the targer.(The foot back can also be used as the kicking part.)

b. The supporting leg stretches its ankle its ankle and knee to help the fore sole pivot the body easily.

c. The kicking leg must stop at the time of kicking the target without making a follow through.

d. Unlike the apchagi or yopchagi, the kicking foot does not make a straight line track. The foot is first raised and then begins to move in a circle.

e. After a hand training, the dollyochagi will be able to make a pounding kick from above the target at the time of kick from above the target at time of kick.

가. 규정동작과 다를 때.

a. Different from the method of the movement.

옆차기 Yop chagi
(Side kick)

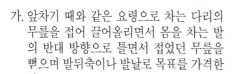

규정동작 Movement 〉

가. 앞차기 때와 같은 요령으로 차는 다리의 무릎을 접어 끌어올리면서 몸을 차는 발의 반대 방향으로 틀면서 접었던 무릎을 뻗으며 발뒤축이나 발날로 목표를 가격한다.

나. 차는 순간 차는 다리의 골반을 엎어지듯 틀면서 고개를 젖혀 차는 목표를 바라본다. 이때 어깨 쪽과 골반 및 다리까지는 나사못 나선과 같이 비틀리는 현상이 일어난다.

다. 찬 다리는 반작용에 의하여 끌어들여 원위치나 마음에 정한 곳에 옮겨놓는다.

라. 딛고 있는 다리는 다리를 끌어올릴 때부터 발목을 충분히 펴서 앞축만 딛고 회전을 빨리 할 수 있게 도와주며, 무릎도 펴서 차는 방향에 추진력을 주어 가속도가 붙게 한다. 찬 다리를 끌어들일 때는 먼저와 같이 발목과 무릎을 낮춘다.

마. 옆차기를 한 순간 상체가 차는 방향 반대쪽(뒤쪽)으로 눕혀져서는 안 된다. 상체가 Y자 모양이 되게 차는 방향으로 중심을 이동시켜 추진력을 증가시킨다. 출발부터 목표까지 일직선이 되어야 한다.

a. As in the apchagi, one lifts up the kicking leg, folding the knee, and then stretches the folded knee as he or she turns the body in the opposite direction to the target and kick the target with the sole of foot.

b. At the moment of the kick, the base of the kicking leg twists at the pelvis in a manner of turning over and the head is raised to keep the eye fixed at the target. At this moment, the trunk also twists like a spiral from the shoulder to the pelvis region and the leg.

c. After the kick, the kicking leg will be drawn back to the original position or where it is intended to placed for next moves.

d. The other leg supporting the body will assist the kick by pivoting on its fore sole, stretching the ankle and help accelerate the speed of kick by stretching knee simultaneously. At the time of retreating the kicking leg. The supporting leg's ankle and knee will lowered again.

e. At the moment of a yopchagi. the upper body should not be left falling in th direction opposite to the target. The upper part of the body must be raised so that the entire body may from a 'Y' letter shape, enabling the weight to bo converted into impellent force of kick.

감점동작의 예 Deduction Factors 〉

가. 규정동작과 다를 때.

a. Different from the method of the movement.

정수기
(Water purifier)

태권도 규정동작
앞치기 (Back fist strike)
얼굴바깥치기 (Outward face back fist strike)

chapter 17

정수기
(Water purifier)

태권도 규정동작

❶ 앞치기　　　❷ 얼굴바깥치기

A : Are you thirsty?

B : Yes. It's too hot and I'm thirsty.

A : Do you want to drink some water?

B : Yes. I'd like to drink cold water.

A : Okay. Let's go to drink water.

본문해석

A : 목마르니?

B : 예. 너무 덥고 목이 말라요.

A : 물 마시고 싶지?

B : 예. 시원한 물을 마시고 싶어요.

A : 좋아. 물 마시러 같이 가자.

○ 다음 문장을 큰 소리로 읽고 따라 쓰세요.

A : Are you thirsty?

_____

B : Yes. It's too hot and I'm thirsty.

_____

A : Do you want to drink some water?

_____

B : Yes. I'd like to drink cold water.

_____

A : Okay. Let's go to drink water.

_____

우리말과 같은 뜻이 되도록 영어 문장을 완성하세요.

01 Are you _____?
(목마르니?)

02 Yes. _____ and I'm thirsty.
(예. 너무 덥고 목이 말라요.)

03 _____ drink some water?
(물 마시고 싶지?)

04 Yes. I'd like to drink _____.
(예. 시원한 물을 마시고 싶어요.)

05 Okay. _____ drink water.
(좋아. 물 마시러 같이 가자.)

쪽지시험

1. water •   • A. 차가운

2. drink •   • B. 마시다

3. cold •   • C. 물

지르기동작

trunk/middle punch	[trʌŋk] / [mídl] [pʌntʃ]	
		몸통지르기
face/high punch	[feis] / [hai] [pʌntʃ]	
		얼굴지르기
regular punch	[régjulər] [pʌntʃ]	바로지르기
reverse punch	[rivə́ːrs] [pʌntʃ]	반대지르기
side punch	[said] [pʌntʃ]	옆지르기
upper punch	[ʌ́pər] [pʌntʃ]	젖혀지르기
round punch	[raund] [pʌntʃ]	돌려지르기

앞치기 Ap chigi
(Back fist strike)

규정동작 Movement

가. 주먹 등의 인지와 중지 부분을 사용한다.
나. 치는 등주먹의 팔목을 구부리면 안 된다.
다. 젖힌 등주먹을 사용한다.
　[요령] 치는 주먹 등을 위로 향하게 하여 반대편 허리(장골능) 위에서 겨드랑이를 스치며 올려 인중 높이로 등주먹을 젖혀 친다.

a. The parts of the pointing finger and middle finger and the middle finger on the fist back are employed.
b. The west on the side of the hitting fist should not be bent.
c. There are an erected fist-back fist and a bent-backward fist-back fist.
[Point of attention] The hitting fist-back fist with its fist-back facing upward is lifted up brushing past the arm-pit over the waist on the opposite to make a hitting by bending the fist-back fist at the height of the philtrum.

감점동작의 예 Deduction Factors

가. 치는 팔이 당기는 팔의 바깥에서 시작할 때.
나. 이 밖에 규정동작이 아닌 행위는 감점이 된다.

a. Attacking arm is performed from outside of the pulling arm.
b. Any other movements other than shown above will be factors of deduction.

태권도 규정동작

얼굴바깥치기 Olgul bakkat chigi
(Outward face back fist strike)

규정동작 Movement

가. 바깥막기와 같은 요령이나 등주먹이 목표인 턱 측면과 관자놀이를 치는 것이다.
나. 관자놀이 높이로 등주먹을 세워서 친다. [요령] 치는 등주먹이 반대편 상완 높이에서 시작해 상대의 관자놀이 높이를 세운 등주먹으로 친다. 치는 등주먹의 팔이 앞치기와 달리, 허리로 당기는 반대 팔의 팔꿈치 밖으로 몸 앞에서 옆 방향으로 원을 그려 나가며 친다. 반대 팔의 주먹은 치는 팔 쪽 어깨선에서 허리로 당긴다.

a. The same way as in the outer-makki, but the hitting is made against the targets of the lateral jaw and the head temple.
b. The fist-back fist is erected the height of the philtrum to deliver a hitting. [Point of attention] The arm that is hitting is to be raised to the height of the opponents eyes, unlike in the Apchigi, make a circular motion from outside the elbow of pulling arm.

감점동작의 예 Deduction Factors

가. 치는 팔이 당기는 팔의 아래와 바깥에서 나올 때.
나. 옆으로 치는 과정에서 팔꿈치가 상하로 움직이는 경우.
다. 이 밖에 규정동작이 아닌 행위는 감점이 된다.

a. Attacking arm coming outside of the pulling arm.
b. Moving the elbow up and down during the process of striking sideway.
c. Any other movements other than shown above will be factors of deduction.

18

취미

(Hobby)

태권도 규정동작
팔굽돌려치기 (Turing elbow strike)

태권도 규정동작

1 팔굽돌려치기

A : What's your hobby?

B : I like playing fun games.

A : What about you?

B : I have many hobbies.

I like computer games in particular.

A : Oh, we have similar hobbies.

본문해석

A : 너는 취미가 뭐니?

B : 나는 재미있는 게임을 하는 거.

A : 너는?

B : 나는 취미가 많아.

특히 컴퓨터 게임을 좋아하지.

A : 우리는 취미가 비슷하구나.

다음 문장을 큰 소리로 읽고 따라 쓰세요.

A : What's your hobby?

_____

B : I like playing fun games.

_____

A : What about you?

_____

B : I have many hobbies.

_____

I like computer games in particular.

_____

A : Oh, we have similar hobbies.

_____

hobby: 취미   like: 좋아하다

many: 많은   particular: 특히

similar: 비슷한, 유사한

우리말과 같은 뜻이 되도록 영어 문장을 완성하세요.

01 _____ hobby?
(너는 취미가 뭐니?)

02 I like playing _____.
(나는 재미있는 게임을 하는 거.)

03 What _____ you?
(너는?)

04 I have _____.
(나는 취미가 많아.)

05 I like computer games _____.
(특히 컴퓨터 게임을 좋아하지.)

06 Oh, we have _____.
(우리는 취미가 비슷하구나.)

1. many •	•	A. 비슷한
2. similar •	•	B. 취미
3. hobby •	•	C. 많은

치기동작

back fist strike	[bæk] [fist] [straik]	앞치기
side strike	[said] [straik]	옆치기
elbow strike	[élbou] [straik]	팔굽치기
knee strike	[niː] [straik]	무릎치기
target strike	[táːrgit] [straik]	표적치기
inward strike	[ínwərd] [straik]	안치기
outward strike	[áutwərd] [straik]	바깥치기
twin side elbow strike	[twin] [said] [élbou] [straik]	멍에치기

팔굽돌려치기 Palkup dollyo chigi
(Turing elbow strike)

규정동작 Movement

가. 돌려 치는 팔꿈치의 손등이 위로 향하게 하
　　고 팔꿈치를 최대한 돌려서 어깨 앞쪽으로
　　오도록 한다.
나. 어깨선보다 팔꿈치가 위쪽에 위치하게 한다.
다. 칠 때 허리를 틀어 준다.

  a. The back of the band looks upward and
　　the elbow is turned to the maximum to
　　be located in from of the shoulder.
  b. The elbow is positioned at a point higher
　　than the shoulder line.
  c. The waist is twisted at the time of hitting.

감점동작의 예 Deduction Factors

가. 허리가 틀어지지 않고 팔꿈치만 돌려 친 경우.
나. 팔꿈치가 어깨보다 내려간 경우.
다. 이 밖에 규정동작이 아닌 행위는 감점이 된다.

  a. Striking only with elbow without twisting
　　the waist.
  b. Striking elbow is lower then the shoulder.
  c. Any other movements other than shown
　　above will be factors of deduction.

전화하기

(Making a phone call)

태권도 규정동작

팔굽옆치기 (Side elbow strike)

chapter 19 전화하기
(Making a phone call)

태권도 규정동작

1 팔굽옆치기

A : Hello, is this the Taekwondo gym?

B : Who's calling, please?

A : Hello, master, this is Joonhyeok.

B : Hi, what's up?

A : I have a cough and have caught a throat cold.
I think I will be able to make it tomorrow to the gym.

B : Okay, take care. See you tomorrow.

본문해석

A : 여보세요, 태권도장이죠?

B : 누구니?

A : 사부님, 준혁이에요.

B : 그래, 무슨 일이니?

A : 제가 기침과 목감기에 걸렸어요. 내일이면 도장에 갈 수 있을 거예요.

B : 그래, 몸조리 잘하고. 내일 보자.

다음 문장을 큰 소리로 읽고 따라 쓰세요.

A : Hello, is this the Taekwondo gym?

_____

B : Who's calling, please?

_____

A : Hello, master, this is Joonhyeok.

_____

B : Hi, what's up?

_____

A : I have a cough and have caught a throat cold.

_____

I think I will be able to make it tomorrow to the gym.

_____

B : Okay, take care. See you tomorrow.

_____

calling: 부름, 외침	cough: 기침하다	see: 보다
throat: 목(구멍)	think: 생각하다	tomorrow: 내일

우리말과 같은 뜻이 되도록 영어 문장을 완성하세요.

01 Hello, is this the _____?
(여보세요, 태권도장이죠?)

02 _____, please?
(누구니?)

03 Hello, _____, this is Joonhyeok.
(사부님, 준혁이에요.)

04 Hi, _____?
(그래, 무슨 일이니?)

05 I have a _____ and have caught a
_____.
(제가 기침과 목감기에 걸렸어요.)

06 I think I will be able to make it _____.
(내일이면 도장에 갈 수 있을 거예요.)

07 Okay, take care. _____.
(그래, 몸조리 잘하고. 내일 보자.)

쪽지시험

1. cough •   • A. 보다

2. see •   • B. 기침하다

3. throat •   • C. 목(구멍)

찌르기동작

upper spear finger thrust	[ʌpər] [spiəːr] [fíŋgər] [θrʌst] 편손끝 젖혀 찌르기	
straight spear finger thrust	[streit] [spiəːr] [fíŋgər] [θrʌst] 편손끝 세워 찌르기	
flat spear finger thrust	[flæt] [spiəːr] [fíŋgər] [θrʌst] 편손끝 엎어 찌르기	
scissors spear finger thrust	[sízəːrz] [spiəːr] [fíŋgər] [θrʌst] 가위손끝 찌르기	
single spear finger thrust	[síŋgl] [spiəːr] [fíŋgər] [θrʌst] 한손끝 찌르기	

팔굽옆치기 Palkup yop chigi
(Side elbow strike)

규정동작 Movement

가. 주춤서기로 치는 팔꿈치의 주먹을 반대편 어깨선까지 가져와서 반대 손바닥에 대고 반대 손이 밀어주는 힘을 이용하여 팔꿈치를 옆으로 친다.

나. 반대 손의 손끝은 위로 향하게 하고 주먹을 잡지 않는다.

다. 반대 손은 치는 팔꿈치 쪽 가슴 앞에 위치시킨다.

a. In a Juchumseogi stance, the fist of hitting side is brought to the shoulder line on the opposite to touch the opposite hand's palm, and then the elbow makes a lateral hitting, making profit of the power of pushing by the opposite hand.

b. The finger-tips of the opposite hand look upward and they do not grab the fist.

c. The opposite hand is positioned in front of the chest on the hitting elbow's side.

감점동작의 예 Deduction Factors

가. 팔꿈치가 어깨선으로 향해 있을 때.

나. 거들어 주는 팔꿈치가 과다하게 들렸을 때.

다. 이 밖에 규정동작이 아닌 행위는 감점이 된다.

a. Elbow facing the line of the shoulder.

b. Assisting arm's elbow is lifted too high.

c. Any other movements other than shown above will be factors of deduction.

스트레스 해소
(Getting rid of stress)

태권도 규정동작

편손끝 세워 찌르기 (Straight spear finger thrust)
편손끝 엎어 찌르기 (Flat spear finger thrust)
편손끝 젖혀 찌르기 (Upper spear finger thrust)

chapter 20

스트레스 해소
(Getting rid of stress)

태권도 규정동작

① 편손끝 세워 찌르기 **②** 편손끝 엎어 찌르기 **③** 편손끝 젖혀 찌르기

A : I'm so stressed out.

B : What's wrong?

A : I'm tired of learning English.
I'm really frustrated.

B : Don't worry.

Let's go to the Taekwondo gym early.

A : That's a good idea. I'm going to get rid of stress,
exercising kicks.

본문해석

A : 나 아주 열 받았어.

B : 무슨 일인데?

A : 영어 배우는 게 이젠 싫증이 나. 정말 스트레스가 쌓여.

B : 걱정하지 마. 우리 태권도장에 얼른 가자.

A : 좋은 생각이야. 발차기로 스트레스를 해소해야지.

다음 문장을 큰 소리로 읽고 따라 쓰세요.

A : I'm so stressed out.

_____

B : What's wrong?

_____

A : I'm tired of learning English.

_____

I'm really frustrated.

_____

B : Don't worry.

_____

Let's go to the Taekwondo gym early.

_____

A : That's a good idea. I'm going to get rid

_____

of stress, exercising kicks.

_____

Key Expressions

wrong: 나쁜, 그릇된　　frustrate: 좌절시키다, 방해하다
exercise: 운동

우리말과 같은 뜻이 되도록 영어 문장을 완성하세요.

01 I'm _____ out.
(나 아주 열 받았어.)

02 What's _____?
(무슨 일인데?)

03 _____ learning English.
(영어 배우는 게 이젠 싫증이 나.)

04 I'm really frustrated.
(정말 스트레스가 쌓여.)

05 _____.
(걱정하지 마.)

06 _____ the Taekwondo gym early.
(우리 태권도장에 얼른 가자.)

07 That's a good idea. I'm going to get rid of stress, _____.
(좋은 생각이야. 발차기로 스트레스를 해소해야지.)

쪽지시험

1. wrong •   • A. 나쁜

2. exercise •   • B. 좌절시키다

3. frustrate •   • C. 운동

차기동작

front kick	[frʌnt] [kik]	앞차기
roundhouse kick	[raundhaus] [kik]	돌려차기
side kick	[said] [kik]	옆차기
ax kick	[æks] [kik]	내려차기
back kick	[bæk] [kik]	뒤차기
crescent kick	[krésənt] [kik]	반달차기
pushing kick	[puʃiŋ] [kik]	밀어차기
jump kick	[dʒʌmp] [kik]	뛰어차기
back spin kick	[bæk] [spin] [kik]	뒤후려차기
front spin kick	[frʌnt] [spin] [kik]	앞후려차기
scissors kick	[sízəːrz] [kik]	가위차기
narae kick	[naːræ] [kik]	나래차기
dolgae kick	[dɔːlgæ] [kik]	돌개차기

편손끝 세워 찌르기 Pyonsonkkeut sewo tzireugi
(Straight spear finger thrust)

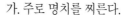

규정동작 Movement

가. 주로 명치를 찌른다.
나. 반대 손의 손등 위로 편손끝 찌르는 팔꿈치
　가 위치한다.
다. 편손끝은 명치 높이로 곧게 찌른다.
　[요령] 반대 손을 펴서 앞으로 뻗은 상태에
　서 팔꿈치를 구부려 손끝이 위로 향하게 한
　다음, 손바닥으로 눌러 막는 동시에 허리에
　있던 편손끝으로 찌른다.

a. This aims mainly at the opponent's solar
plexus.
b. The elbow of the hand making a
pyonsonkkeut tzireugi rests over the
hand-back of the hand.
c. The pyonsonkkeut(Palm-fist finger-
tips) makes a tzireugi straight forward
in parallel with the height of the solar
plexus.
[Point of attention] In a state in which
he other hand is unfolded and extended
forward, the elbow will be bent making
finger-tips look upward and then a
pushing-makki by the palm and a
pyonsonkkeut tzireugi from the waist are
executed simultaneously.

감점동작의 예 Deduction Factors

가. 규정동작과 다를 때.
a. Different from the method of the movement.

편손끝 엎어 찌르기 Pyonsonkkeut upeo tzireugi
(Flat spear finger thrust)

규정동작 Movement

가. 주로 눈, 목, 명치를 찌른다.
　[요령] 찌르는 손등이 위를 향하게 하여 손
　끝으로 찌른다.
a. This is mainly used in attacking the
　opponent's eyes, neck and solar plexus.
　[Point of attention] Make the back of the
　thrusting hand face upwards and thrust
　with the fingertips.

감점동작의 예 Deduction Factors

가. 규정동작과 다를 때.
a. Different from the method of the movement.

편손끝 젖혀 찌르기 Pyonsonkkeut jeocho tzireugi
(Upper spear finger thrust)

규정동작 Movement

가. 주로 늑골, 명치, 샅 등을 찌른다.
나. 손끝을 아래로 하여 손바닥 부분이 위로 향하게 한다.
다. 반대 손은 바닥 부분을 얼굴 방향으로 하여 어깨 높이로 올린다.
[요령] 찌르는 손은 허리에서 손등이 위로 향하게 하고, 반대 손은 앞으로 뻗어 손등이 위로 향하게 한 후 교차하여 찌른다.

a. This is mainly used in attacking the opponent's ribs, solar plexus, groin and etc.
b. The finger-tips will look downward while the palm side will face upward.
c. The opposite hand, whose base part looks toward the face, is raised up to the level of the shoulder.
[Point of attention] The hand making jireugi rests on the waist with its palm facing upward, and opposite hand is extended forward, with its back of the hand looking upward, to deliver tzireugi alternately together with the before-mentioned.

감점동작의 예 Deduction Factors

가. 규정동작과 다를 때.
a. Different from the method of the movement.

저자 소개 >>

최원교

1976년 수원 태생으로 경희대학교 태권도학과를 졸업하고 성균관대학교 과학기술대학원에서 석사학위를 취득했다. 대학에서 태권도시범론 겸임교수로 재임한 바 있으며, 현재 태권도장과 1인 지식기업 에듀컬연구소를 운영하고 있다.
벤처경진상 수상 경험과 발명특허 취득을 바탕으로 태권도를 수련 중인 어린이들의 학습에 도움을 주고자 태권도를 이용한 학습법 개발에 몰두하고 있다.

저서로는 『발표와 한자 내 손안에』, 『비만클리닉』, 『태권한자 연구논문』, 『자기경영 성공전략』, 『최원교 사부와 함께하는 태권영어교실』, 『태권한자카드세트』(출간 예정), 『최원교 사부와 함께하는 태권한자교실』(출간 예정) 등이 있으며 현재 다양한 학습교재들을 집필 중에 있다.

참고문헌 a bibliography

국기원, 『태권도교본』, 오성출판사, 2006.
세계태권도연맹, 『품새 규정 동작 해설』, 2007.
대한태권도협회, 『품새 경기 규칙』, 2006.
『열린태권도연구소 교육자료집』, 2001.
『초등 필수 영단어집』, 좋은 글 어학연구소, 2004.

 최원교 사부와 함께하는
태권영어교실

초판인쇄 | 2009년 1월 5일
초판발행 | 2009년 1월 10일

지은이 | 최원교
펴낸이 | 채종준
펴낸곳 | 한국학술정보(주)
주 소 | 경기도 파주시 교하읍 문발리 513-5 파주출판문화정보산업단지
전 화 | 031)908-3181(대표)
팩 스 | 031)908-3189
홈페이지 | http://www.kstudy.com
E-mail | 출판사업부 publish@kstudy.com

등 록 | 제일산-115호(2000. 6. 19)
가 격 | 11,000원

ISBN 978-89-534-0544-8 63740 (Paper Book)
      978-89-534-0546-2 68740 (e-Book)